Taking Flight
STANDING STILL

Taking Flight
STANDING STILL

*Teaching Toward Poetic and Imaginative
Understanding*

RICHARD LEWIS

Touchstone Center Publications
New York

in collaboration with

Codhill Press
New Paltz

Taking Flight, Standing Still
© 2010 by Richard Lewis

The author and publisher have made every effort to contact the following publishers - and gratefully acknowledge their permission to reprint the following material:

"Night Rain at Guang-Kou" by Yang Wan-li from *Heaven My Blanket, Earth My Pillow: Poems from Sung Dynasty China by Yang Wang-Li,* translated by Jonathan Chaves. Published by Weatherhill, Inc., 1975.

"Not Knowing/The Name of the Tree" from *The Narrow Road to the Deep North and Other Travel Sketches* by Matsuo Basho translated with an introduction by Nobuyuki Yuasa. Penguin Classics,1966. Copyright © Nobuyuki Yuasa, 1966.

"How can you gather together" by George Seferis from *George Seferis, Collected Poems (1924-1955)* translated, edited and introduced by Edmund Keely and Philip Sherrard. Published by Princeton University Press, 1971.

"Dance of the Animals" from *The African Saga* by Blaise Cendras. Published by Greenwood Press Reprint, 1969.

"Follow the stream" by Cid Corman from *Aegis: Selected Poems, 1970 -1980 by Cid Corman.* Published by Station Hill Press, 1983. © Cid Corman, 1983.

Cover and book design by Heidi Neilson

Cover drawing by Shawntey, second grade, and title page drawing by Joevanni, second grade, PS 20, Manhattan, New York. Drawing on Page 117 by an anonymous child, third grade, PS 56, Queens, New York.

Library of Congress Control Number: 2009941764

ISBN: 9781929299089

Publication of this book was made possible, in part, by a grant to The Touchstone Center for Children from the New York State Council on the Arts.

Touchstone Center Publications
141 East 88th Street
New York, NY 10128
www.touchstonecenter.net

Codhill Press
1 Arden Lane
New Paltz, NY 12561
CodhillPress@aol.com

*To the many dedicated and gifted
artists, teachers and administrators
I have had the honor and pleasure
of collaborating with*

and

*to those many children who were
always themselves—and shared with us their
vision and wonderment, the beauty and
poetry of their imagining worlds.*

—R.L.

BOOKS BY RICHARD LEWIS

From the Sleep of Waters, Illustrated by Susan Share, 2010

Sea Tale, Illustrated by Gigi Alvaré, 2009

Shaking the Grass for Dew: Poems by Richard Lewis, 2008

I Catch My Moment: Art and Writing by Children on the Life of Play, 2007

A Tree Lives, Illustrated by Noah Baen, 2005

CAVE: An Evocation of the Beginnings of Art, Illustrated by Elizabeth Crawford and George Hirose, 2003

The Bird of Imagining, Illustrated by Children from New York City
Public Schools, 2002

In the Space of the Sky, Illustrated by Debra Frasier, 2002

Each Sky Has Its Words, Illustrated by Gigi Alvaré, 2000

Living By Wonder: Essays on the Imaginative Life of Childhood, 1998

When Thought Is Young: Reflections on Teaching and the Poetry of the Child, 1992

All of You Was Singing: A Retelling of an Aztec Myth, Illustrated by Ed Young, 1991

In the Night Still Dark: A Retelling of the Hawaiian Creation Chant,
Illustrated by Ed Young, 1988

The Luminous Landscape: Chinese Art and Poetry, 1981

I Breathe a New Song: Poems of the Eskimo, Introduction by Edmund Carpenter,
Illustrated by Oonark, 1971

There Are Two Lives: Poems by Children of Japan, Co-edited and translated
by Haruna Kimura, 1970

The Way of Silence: Prose and Poetry of Basho, Photographs by Helen Buttfield, 1970

Still Waters of the Air: Three Modern Spanish Poets, 1970

Muse of the Round Sky: Greek Lyric Poetry, 1969

Journeys: Prose by Children of the English-Speaking World, 1969

Of This World: A Poet's Life in Poetry - Poetry of Issa,
Photographs by Helen Buttfield, 1969

The Park, Photographs by Helen Buttfield, 1968

Out of the Earth I Sing: Poetry and Songs of Primitive Peoples of the World, 1968

The Wind and The Rain: Poems by Children, Photographs by Helen Buttfield, 1968

Miracles: Poems by Children of the English-Speaking World, 1968

Moon, For What Do You Wait? Poetry by Tagore, Illustrated by Ashley Bryan, 1967

In A Spring Garden: A Selection of Haiku Poetry, Illustrated by Ezra Jack Keats, 1965

The Moment of Wonder: A Collection of Chinese and Japanese Poetry, 1964

In Praise of Music, 1963

Table of Contents

To the Reader

I OFTEN STRUGGLE, as we all do, in explaining the imagination. And I continue to rephrase and revise what I mean by poetry and the poetic experience. In some ways both qualities of thought are a lifetime challenge to understand—and even then they remain hauntingly difficult to articulate.

That of course is their attraction and importance. Like all species that grow and die they evolve—and if one considers their history, it is clear that they too refuse to remain always the same for each of us.

In two prior books, *When Thought Is Young* and *Living By Wonder*, I brought together writings that focused, from the perspective of both a parent and teacher, on the roots and growth of the poetic and imaginative in childhood. This book is similar as a means of sharing more recent ways of interpreting the probings, questions and sources of understandings that have been crucial to my working as a teaching-artist, with children and adults, particularly through the arts and education projects of The Touchstone Center for Children, an organization in New York City I founded in 1969 and continue to direct.

Over the years the major focus of the Center has been the life of the imagination and its relation to the natural world. This intersection between what we speak of as "nature" and what we mean by our "imagination" has resulted in projects in schools that have explored themes and images based on natural phenomena: from stones and trees, to birds and languages, to shells and dreams. In large part, I, in collaboration with other teaching artists of the Center, wanted to find that point where the imagination, and its expressive and artistic capacities, could be at the very core of our ability to perceive and understand. We wanted to make apparent that somewhere in this meeting place between our imagination and aliveness, something of the poetic nature of ourselves exists —and is pivotal to our sense of learning and knowing.

Like one of the many flying creatures we spent time imagining and dreaming with, I have constructed *Taking Flight, Standing Still* so it too has its moments of flight and stillness. Each of the descriptive pieces are offset by a page of short, aphoristic writings selected from notes to myself, often late at night or early in the morning, after working with children and teachers in a classroom. The notes are meant to be a quiet, evocative counterpoint to some of the ideas the longer pieces might suggest. Only in the first piece, *In the Meadow of Our Thoughts,* have I included more extensive reflective comments within the overall narrative.

While not a formal outline of how to teach, or a practical guide for the creation of a curriculum, this book, if only as a personal exploration, will be part of our continuing discussion of the urgent need to bring the arts—and our innate expressive and imaginative abilities—into the mainstream of education. It is my hope that it will serve as a modest reminder of the importance of preserving the language of childhood in ourselves, so we might be better able to encourage and protect the doing and making, playing and imagining that has always been the profound and generous conversation of all children.

The moonlight
Seeps through the
Pebble
Sunlight pushes its
Way toward the
Stone
They meet in the
middle and Shine a
Song.

-Emma, Age 7

Firstly, this provocation of wonder
—and of course, lastly.

Language is the imagination.
The desire to speak is to imagine.

Questions I ask of children—of myself, really.

I want to be an advocate of the immeasurable.

As you teach, unlearn what teaching is—take a chance—
begin at the beginning.

In the Meadow of Our Thoughts

SOME CLASSROOMS where I work are very noisy. Not necessarily the shouting-match kind of noise—but classrooms filled with children who like talking, and who use words as levers of contact. If you're not used to it, the noise can seem chaotic and not very productive. But if you listen long enough, you can hear sound patterns that resonate with children's thoughts being tried out. Occasionally the noise level becomes difficult to tolerate. Then I, or the classroom teacher, ask for a moment of quiet so we can proceed. On the whole, the noise is just enough for us to talk through and above, and just enough to know that here are children who, in their exuberance to speak, are enjoying every ounce of their talking.

A room of this kind where we can be surrounded by the rich environment of "talking" noise is like a fertile garden where everything is in a state of perpetual blossoming. I remember fondly one such class I had the good fortune of working in, a first grade class in one of New York City's oldest public schools, in the borough of Queens.

Come join me, look over my shoulder, as I go back in time to re-enter that classroom.

The hallways have dark-stained wooden floors that creak incessantly from armies of children who walked over them for many years. When I go in, I am greeted by children. Even though they have never seen me before, they immediately rush up and want me to become a part of their life—right here and now.

"My mommy's havin' a baby. She's in the hospital."

"I have a cat named Clarence."

"My teacher doesn't like kids who spit food out."

"Who are you? What are you doing here?"

I can hardly keep up with their talking. Seeing me a bit befuddled, one of the children comes up and takes me by the hand, leading me to her desk. Carefully, so no one else will notice, she takes out a piece of paper on which she has scribbled a few words. She whispers in my ear, but I don't really understand. It is a major secret that I am to keep for her. Assured I will keep it, she goes her way and continues a conversation on the other side of the room.

Meantime, the teacher, Ms. Golden, a seasoned, caring listener, comes over to me. We introduce ourselves and she in turn brings the class to a moment of seeming stillness.

"Children, we have a special guest today who wants to talk to you. He wants very, very much to share something with you. So would you all please come sit down on the rug with him and give him your attention."

The murmurs continue for a while as the children come and sit close to me. A few furtively steal a glance at me, wondering who I am and what I am going to do.

I've often been asked what it is that I do. Going into classrooms and talking to children about an old leaf I saw on the ground, or the colorful bird that flew overhead while I was walking, might seem to be small matters within the larger demands of learning.

Sometimes before my arrival in a classroom, teachers tell the children that a "poet" or a special visitor is coming to the room. Expecting something different from the usual day-to-day activities, the children are not quite sure what I am really up to. They are often surprised when I take from my bag a bird's feather, or a fallen twig.

Perhaps to these children I'm a botanist who likes poems. Maybe I've simply come to play and talk about birds and trees. Whatever they think of me, in time we soon become engaged in a process of imagining and expression which, if not delighting them, at least baffles a few enough to elicit strong responses.

I must admit that when I was younger, I had no idea that my occupation would be what it has become. In retrospect, it's quite clear that what I do is a legitimate way of spending one's life. When children ask me if I get paid for this kind of work, and I say that I do, a number of them are very puzzled and find it difficult to fit me into a familiar occupation.

This question of my own work-identity is a fascinating one. It raises a more substantive group of questions as to the role and place of the artist, the poet, the imaginer, the dreamer in each of us in our culture. And this question, in turn, brings us full circle to the meaning of our human ability to imagine and create.

Why do we create? Why is it necessary to imagine? Will our imagining help us or hinder us? Is the making of art important to our survival? As the world turns upon its axis, and we enter another millennium somewhat dazed and confused by the previous one, shouldn't these questions be the most important ones we continue to think upon?

The children in front of me pay as much attention to my hands as they do my eyes. They watch closely as I rub my hands. And as I begin to speak, I continue to rub my hands.

"It's very nice to be here today. How are you all this morning?" I ask. Of course I hear in return not the usual "I'm well, thank you," but "My daddy said he was going to buy me a bicycle," or "Our canary got away yesterday," or "My dog doesn't like Miffy."

"Who is Miffy?" I inquire.

"You know, my goldfish," is shot right back to me by a child sitting cross-legged in the middle of the group.

After a few more of the children tell me not so much how they are but what is on their minds, I ask each one his or her name. Many giggles and laughter follow when I mispronounce a name, and I feel silly for not knowing how. But I make no bones about being ignorant—or silly. And they continue to laugh at me whenever I trip over a "Vladimir" or a "Jesus."

They are still watching my hands as I go back to the boy who said that his canary got away yesterday.

"Where did it go?" I ask.

"It flew around the room and got stuck on the lamp shade."

"You mean it got really stuck?"

"Yeah, it couldn't move, so it got stuck."

"Maybe it was scared."

"Yeah, maybe…"

"I wonder," I say to the whole group of children, "if we were that canary and we got stuck on the lamp shade, I wonder if we could unstick ourselves from the lamp shade and fly around the room, maybe thinking it is the sky, and we could look at clouds and the sun and the moon and the stars…"

I don't know where or how, but as a young child, I became fascinated with birds. Not as specimens or types, but as creatures hovering above and around me. A bird was something I could watch —as some children might watch hours of a baseball game, waiting for the moment that would totally engage them. For me, though, it was the mixture of predictability and the unknown that seemed to be part of how a bird grazed the sky.

Somehow a bird connoted a life different from my own, but one strangely similar. I envied birds, and yearned to be like them. This fascination, which became a secret I could hardly understand, was apparent whenever I went to the beach. As a serious nine- or ten-year-old I would sit attentively on a mound of warm sand and watch the racings of the sand plovers as they skipped back and forth with each wave.

We cannot really say why something becomes a vivid memory or why we have particular memories that become decisive entry points into a rich font of associations and feelings. In my case, I suspect there was a sensation, a feeling that what I was watching was more than just a group of birds, but a way of experiencing wonder —a wonder that was a marking for the way I would perceive myself in relation to the living, breathing world.

Noticing that a number of children are still looking at my hands, I continue to talk about our "unstuck bird." Quite deliberately then, I begin to slowly open my hands a very small amount. Gesturing with one hand to the opening that my other hand is shaping, I say: "Maybe inside here, inside this hand, maybe I have a little bit of the sky. Not a whole lot, but a little—just enough to mix some air together so a few clouds can come alive. Maybe if I look inside my hand I can find a star—or if I'm real lucky the moon and the sun…maybe, maybe…"

By now some children are wondering what this is about. As with every group, a few naysayers question this free-wheeling imagining. I purposely pick one hesitant child, Margaret, to come and help me look inside my hand. Margaret is neatly dressed— and she has a quiet glint in her eyes.

"What do you see, Margaret, when you look inside my hand? Can you see anything—anything moving or stirring, the way wind does when it gets a little restless?"

Margaret looks into my hand, keeping one eye on me and my hand and the other eye on what her classmates are doing. Looking inside, she turns to me and with a six-year-old's way of being shy, says in a soft, hardly audible voice, "Nothing…"

"Nothing?" I respond. "Well, that's something, isn't it? Margaret, look again," I ask, "and see if in the nothing—something is beginning to move."

She peers once more into the half-opened hand—and this time looks back at me and shakes her head, an all-knowing but gentle "No."

"Margaret, you know what I'm going to do? I'm going to ask you to take a little of the air around you in this room, roll it up into a ball, and put it into my hand. I know when you do this, it will get the 'nothing' inside going. And if we are patient, maybe in the nothing there will be a little bit of the sky."

She agrees to help me. And as I hold her arm she opens her hand and cautiously takes some of the air. Talking to her through this simple gesture (she rolls it carefully into a small ball) I say, "Don't let it fall, Margaret…be careful…" I turn to the rest of the children and ask if anyone else can take some air and roll it up in a ball. Practically everyone wants to do that; in fact, most children can't wait to do everything that Margaret is doing. So I ask a group of three or four of them to come and join Margaret and myself. And up they come, bouncing every step, excited by the prospect of becoming part of our new adventure.

With Margaret next to me, the other children take the air around them. With their fistfuls of compacted air, they come to me and deposit their new-found treasures into my half-opened hand. We wait. I close my eyes. I speak to all the children in a suspended whisper:

"Would everyone please close their eyes and look at the night behind your eyes. Don't say anything, but look closely behind the night; and when you can see a few stars, climb the sky inside your eyes. Be very quiet. And when I say 'Whewwwww.....' open your eyes..."

The room is very still. Again I say "Whewwwwww..." And one by one the children open their eyes. I ask Margaret if she can see in the "nothing" of my hand just a little, a very small part of the sky. She bends close. I bring my hand close to her eyes—and taking a deep breath she nods "Yes."

Some sensations, memorized into our bodies since earliest childhood, must be what we experienced when we first realized the sky's existence. But at first, in our infant's stare, the shapes and textures and smells of our mother's and our father's bodies must have been our knowable horizon—until we dared to look beyond. And soon the room we awoke in, and the light defining its presence, was another horizon we took into ourselves. Eventually, going outside, we saw the sky. Its distance between ourselves and what we could grasp and see of it must have seemed immense.

We have begun to make the sky. Margaret, who was unsure of her imagining, is beaming now that she has let go of a stubborn part of what she thought might be the right answer. I'm beaming too because we have done this together, and Margaret's consenting to be playful with me has made it possible for us, and the rest of the class, to adventure further. And so on we go.

I immediately ask the children to find the sky in one of their hands, and to begin to draw a picture of it with their free hand.

We take enough sky to fill three rooms. When we have exhausted ourselves, and perhaps the sky, we form a big circle. Making sure every corner, every niche, every hidden crevice is covered with the sky, we lift it up into the classroom with one big collective sigh. Then, as is appropriate, we rest.

Sitting in a big circle we shake our hands out, joggle our heads, and start to discuss a serious matter. "Now that we have our sky, how are we going to see what's up there and down here? What can we do to get some light?"

"The sun, the sun!" is the responding chorus.

"And where should we put it?" I query.

"Over there, over there!" they shout. So the children and I make the sun with our bare hands until it gets too heavy. I ask a few children to help, as we lift this molten beam of light up - up to the ceiling in the corner of the room.

"That was a load, wasn't it?"

Everyone agrees.

We then go on to the moon. Caressing the night darkness, we shape another beam of light so we can see where we are going, and hang it on the other side of the room. We take stars from our glowing fingers and hang them throughout the sky. We bend down; and from all the blossoming flowers at our feet, we gather the exuberant reds and blues, greens and yellows, and with an excited flourish of our hands, we shower the sky with a splendid rainbow. To celebrate, we jump up and down, take a deep breath, and in one exalted leap of faith, exhale clouds of every shape into our expectant sky.

We have no proof of what we did, as young children, to make the distance between ourselves and the sky closer. For the sake of discussion, let us say we may have populated the world around us with whatever objects we were surrounded with—a chair, a table, a bed, our favorite stuffed animal—and if we were fortunate enough, the sight of a leafing tree, a busy squirrel, or a flower's bent-over salute.

Perhaps because the tree, the squirrel, and the flower manifested different qualities of life from the chair, the table, and the bed, they became part of the landscape we began to know as living like ourselves. Such perceiving of what is alive may have been the beginnings of our seeing ourselves in partnership with what is also alive around us. Added to this perception was our growing awareness of being accepted into life—our being touched, spoken to, held close— human expressions of love which made it possible to populate our inner sense of ourselves with all that responds and reacts.

So the tree, the squirrel, and the flower, which also reacted, became attributes of what we ourselves also were and did. Our inner landscape became ever so gradually and subtly the place we knew to be ourselves and could find comfort and reassurance in. Like the adult's hand we held tightly, this inner landscape, and the images it represented, was our guide to the world existing between ourselves and the sky.

With the time I am to spend today with the class almost over, and knowing that I will have the opportunity of returning at least four more times in the coming weeks, I pass out paper, pencils, and oil crayons to the children so they can draw a picture of the sky they have just created. Soon the children's skyful world begins to appear—dictated, so to speak, from themselves to the empty space of paper in front of them. Before I leave the room I ask of the children one last thing:

"Will everyone please look up at the sky and with your right hand touch a little bit of the air the sky breathes, and a little bit of the light the sky gives, and bring them carefully into your other hand. Listen to them, and then send them back into your sky." As I say all of this, slowly their small hands touch and grasp the invisible air and light, and bring them to their ears—and like dancers of another time, the children pirouette their invisibilities back onto the ceiling of the room.

After so many years, I can still recall the voices of my parents when I was three as they closed windows before an impending hurricane; looking down as an eight-year-old from a huge boulder into clear streamwater and seeing my reflection and the shape of a startled fish, crisscrossing; as a ten-year-old, being alone in a canoe on a deserted lake. These memories are as clear to me as the moment they happened, not only in details but in the feelings and sensations they evoked.

Why do such memories persist? Do they linger because we hold onto them as part of the map of our consciousness; or do they stay because they are, in themselves, meaningful to us as particular instances of our need to feel integrated into a presence larger than our own?

Strange questions, these, for they seem as we ask them to bring back the nature of childhood—and those discoveries we often dismiss as not being learning. They are, as we look at them, not the cleanly-scrubbed facts we were told it would be best to learn in school in order to gain more facts. They are not even the memories we can share in a relaxed social setting, or that may have provoked a great fear or sadness. They are, it seems to me, undercurrents of a much larger body of thought.

Perhaps they were expressions of a wonder more akin to poetic, intuitive learning. And perhaps this poetic learning is at the base of other learning—for, as a way of knowing, it is the process and

means by which we acquire information through what our senses,
when fully engaged, can bring to wonderment. This kind of learning
seems to involve a world charged with a dynamic presence known
from within ourselves.

During the week, when I think about the class of first-grade
children, I again reflect upon the noise that emanates from their
busy room. It is a room in startling contrast to others in the
school, where there is either polite and mandated silence, or the
haphazard noise of restless children struggling with their own
fears and vulnerability.

The noise of "my" classroom is closer to music, to sounds
rising and falling in harmony with what the children happen to
be doing at the moment. If they are sitting listening to a story being read by their teacher, there is the sound of someone agreeing
or disagreeing with the story or anticipating where it might be
going. There is the sound of conversations as they draw pictures.
And when they are absorbed and somehow satisfied by the pleasure of their own concentration, a singing might arise from no-
where. Always there is the sound of small children moving about,
their feet often in untied shoes, shuffling across the floor.

And if we listen intently, we hear the sounds of a deeper intelligence of their dreaming minds, wandering from here to there
as if carried by the wind, pollinating whatever thought is avail-
able at the moment. We enter the room as fellow noisemakers,
engaged in the way the sounds of our minds constantly interrupt
us because there is much to see and hear.

The logic of the sounds is not straightforward, but again like
music, in which a new phrase or melody can suddenly backtrack
or leap forward from the simplest of rhythms or cluster of notes.
These are sounds more improvisational than preconceived. To be

with children, you have to play with their noise, to join in where their sounds are clustering—and learn to dance their dance.

For my second visit the following week, I open the door just enough to see if it is all right to come in, enough to give *just* the right amount of space for a child with a pair of sparrow eyes to see me and come running over to the door announcing to everyone else: "He's here…Richard's here. What'd ya bring, Richard?"

Before I can get the door all the way open, Sparrow Eyes gives me a big hug and tugs me by the arm to come in. Another child comes running over and wants to take my bag and my coat. By this time, "noise" has fluttered carelessly from everywhere, and Ms. Golden, with her magical override of a voice, summons all the children to gather on the rug where we met last time.

The rich accumulation of feelings, images, and ideas we have learned during any period of our lives are, for all intents and purposes, the landscapes we inhabit. Throughout days to come, these landscapes change and fashion us accordingly.

Such a landscape is the poetic world we build in us so that we might comprehend the world existing outside of us. Why poetic? Because, as with the original meaning of poetry—"to make"—we are making and remaking ourselves. In short, then, this, our most precious learning, emanates from the poetry on which we build our lives and consciousness.

Sitting in front of me once again, the children are eager to hear what I am about to say, and I am eager to see if they remember what we did last week. A week is a long time in a child's life. As with us in our busy worlds, they are immersed in a daily battle of details to which they are required to pay attention. For them to recall how we made our sky is something I do not want to take for granted. I am careful to ease back into the sky with a reference to the weather outside. Because it has been raining for a few days, I say to the group:

"Did anyone get wet when it rained on Tuesday?"

A few hands go up, and I ask one child in the back to tell us.

"I got wet," said Jimmy. "My mommy didn't give me an umbrella. When I got to school my shoes were wet—and my socks too."

"Did you see the rain?" I reply.

"No."

"Did you feel the rain?"

"A little bit…"

"What did it feel like?"

"I don't know…"

"Did it feel wet?"

"A little bit…"

Realizing that Jimmy needs a bit of encouragement to expand on his feelings, I ask, "Has anyone else seen or felt the rain? Can you show us with your hands what the rain looked like when it fell? Jimmy, will you come up and sit with me so you can show us how to catch some rain as it falls down." Jimmy comes over to me, and soon I have a small group showing us the falling rain. Their hands pencil the empty space in front of them as their fingers move leisurely back and forth. I put out my arm so the children can have the rain fall on me, and I beckon Jimmy to do the same thing.

"Can you feel the rain now, Jimmy?"

"Yeah," nodding his head confidently.

"What does it feel like?"

Thinking for a minute, he says, "Like little dots—sort of…"

"Where's the rain coming from?"

"Up there—in the sky," Jimmy says, pointing to the sky we made last week.

"Up there…in our sky, in the sky we made…?" I ask, gesturing to the same place.

"Yeah…"

I ask everyone who helped us to sit down while I mime making an umbrella with my hands. I open it, lift it above my head, and begin to walk under the sky. I move it slightly to my left and peer up. "But where's the sun?"

"Over there, over there!" in a chorus of adamant recognition—gesturing to the spot we had placed it the week before.

"And where's the moon?"

The same chorus shouts out, "Over there!"—annoyed this time that I can't remember such an important thing as where we had put the moon. I provocatively point to a slightly different place from where the children are gesturing. No sooner do I do this than they, exasperated, point to the exact place we had placed the moon. Nothing has been forgotten. The stars and the clouds and the rainbow are where we had put them. Nothing has moved—including the children's delight in showing me precisely where everything should be in *our sky*. There it is, visible only to the children in this classroom, hanging proudly from the peeling plaster of the classroom ceiling with its modern light fixtures glimmering pale fluorescent shadows.

If our senses are pivotal to knowing, the sources of our imagining are not simply in the brain alone, but in the fiber of our ability to touch, to feel, to hear, and to see. While these abilities might be controlled and ultimately made known to us by the mechanism of our brain, isn't it possible that every part of our body has a way to feel and understand a knowledge specific to itself?

Does a hand, for example, have the ability to imagine within its circumference? Maybe then our bodies are filled with a multitude of imagining networks. Since science cannot yet tell us what exactly the imagination is, is there not room enough for us to determine the meaning and function of imaginative thought?

Today is going to be a day of visits. The sun is going to visit the moon, the clouds are going to visit the rainbow, the sun is going to visit the stars. Since the sky is in place, I hope that we can begin letting the children move the various parts of it as if they were neighbors visiting each other. We clear some of the desks and the furniture from the center of the room, and ask all the children to stand in a big circle as we did the week before. I search for a few volunteers to play the various parts of the sky. (Never a problem getting volunteers, since it seems that children are fearless actors always ready to appear on a stage.)

Within seconds, we have a contingent of moons and suns and clouds and rainbows. I suggest that we dance first—the moon to dance as the moon might dance, and the sun to dance as the sun might dance, and so on. Of course there is some initial overexuberance, but I restrain it by putting us all into "slow motion." As graceful as the orbiting planets themselves, the children twirl and spin, circle upon circle, occasionally letting their fingers touch the fingers of another constellation close by. When we get used to this celestial dance, I ask them to add a humming sound to their encircling, and for those children who are not actively moving to add their own sky-hum. The room at this moment is transfixed, if rooms can be transfixed. Even the papers on the desks seem especially alert.

We repeat this dance a number of times so that all the children will have a chance to make a visit. When we finish, we give out some paper so the children can draw what the sky looked like when all the visits were taking place. We also ask the children, if they feel comfortable doing so, to write a few words about what happened when they paid a visit in the sky. For those children who can't yet write, we say that we—Ms. Golden, a student teacher, and myself—will come by to help.

After receiving the paper, crayons, and pencils, the children scatter to various parts of the room. Some go back to their desk, others find privacy under a table, some sit in the middle of the space we danced in, and others burrow behind a stray pillow or the leg of a chair.

There is always noise as children go into themselves and find the images they wish to draw or speak about. It is the noise of the children's uncertainty as to how these images might appear. It is also the noise of a welling excitement in other children as they continue being inside the images they have imagined. The chatter and banter is a reassuring sign that our imagining is a part of the whole spectrum of the day. To talk about other things beside what it is they are drawing and, in some cases, writing, is not necessarily a sign of distraction, but an indication that children need to mix the mundane with the imagined. While Ms. Golden and I have the adult urge to tell the children to "Please be quiet," we wisely refrain because despite the rush of babbling noise, the children are busy getting their images onto paper.

I walk around the room peering over the shoulders of my sky people. From my perspective, I see vibrant suns meeting clouds, quarter moons hanging from the arc of a rainbow, and stars swerving out of the darkness. I watch Jasmine as she fills up her paper with a dazzling yellow interrupted by white clouds. She draws with the intensity of someone who knows what she wants to do, with hardly a pause in her effort to get down all that she is seeing. I don't want to interrupt her, but a while later I come back and sit down on the floor with her.

"I bet you know a lot about those clouds. And all that sunlight…"

"Yep…"

"Could you tell me what you know, because I'd like to write it down for you."

"Well," she said, not stopping what she is drawing, "the sunshine got together…" I write quickly, but not quickly enough before she says the next part of the sentence, "…with the cloud."

"Hold on a second, Jasmine; I need to catch up with you." I write down the whole sentence, and then repeat it back to her. "The sunshine got together with the cloud." She listens carefully and nods her approval. Then, looking at me to see if I am ready, she continues: "But when the cloud…saw the wind…they got scared." I write this down as fast as I can, but before I know it she is already onto the next sentence.

"Then they got…"

"Hold on, Jasmine—you're faster than your wind!" She smiles, and waits while I write. Finally I say to her, "Then they got…" and she echoes me, saying, "Then they got together and…" in a matter-of-fact voice, she concludes simply, "fell in love."

I get the word "love" inscribed just in time, because Jasmine is about to get up and get another piece of paper, for another meeting of the elements. I urge her to wait while I read back what she has told me. She agrees and we huddle, as if in deep discussion, while I read her story back to her:

"The sunshine got together with the cloud. But when the cloud saw the wind, they got scared. Then they got together, and they fell in love."

Somewhere in our past, we realized that we could, willfully and consciously, create images that were like beacons of light within the surrounding darkness of our inward selves. We were dreamers who partook of the logic of our dreaming in order to understand the logic of the universe we lived in, and so imagined, fashioning significant images of our own that became, astonishingly, a language we could communicate to ourselves and others.

Survival became dependent on our ability to imagine food and shelter. We could bring them into being by our gift of seeing beyond our immediate instinctive reactions, so that we could plan by imagining possibilities for our future. Our survival was equally dependent on how well we could create, by making images inside of ourselves. Thoughts and feelings gave us personal meanings. Both forms of imagining were perhaps the key to how brilliantly and profoundly human life eventually evolved—a sense of what we can do to make our bodies survive, and what we can do to make our personhood survive.

Aside from the ebb and flow of the "noise" in the classroom, something else seems to run through the mood of the room itself. As I continue to go around listening to and writing down what the children are thinking, I hear affectionate thoughts about what the elements of the sky mean. For instance, Tino, drawing a picture of a round, buoyant cloud, leans up to me and says, quite unabashedly: "I love you cloud, with my love…" and Hamid, with curiosity sparking from his eyes, whispers: "The stars getting married? Do they kiss?"

There seems to be a quiet undercurrent of human love circulating in our sky. And why not? These are children who, given the support of their teacher, are embracing the world around them, with the attributes they ask of it. And if, through their imaginations, they imagine the sky and its attendant parts to be natural extensions of their need to love and be loved, then to express this love towards the stars and clouds is a perfectly obvious occurrence.

After twenty minutes of drawing and thinking about the ways that our sky can socialize, we gather back on the rug and share a few of the drawings and thoughts. Like the first time, we dance our hands in a farewell gesture to our sky.

"Will everybody take some of the moon's light in one hand, and some of the sun's light in the other, and introduce them to each other. When they know each other better, introduce yourself to them. Then scatter them back into our sky.... Thank you, everyone."

After I speak with Ms. Golden, the last thing I see as I leave the room is one of the children standing by a window looking up. Because she is small and the window high, she can see only a narrow passageway of light coming through the rooftops of the tenement buildings next door to the school.

On the bus and subway back to my home, I write a few notes about the class. It's not always easy to remember every detail; a part of me would prefer only to savor again the playful feelings of reaching into the sky, or dancing, or becoming the sun or the moon.

Unable to find a seat on the subway, I let myself ride the motion of the train. Daydreaming, as I often do, I find that the children of the classroom sky keep reassembling themselves in my thoughts. I think about the child standing near the window. What has she been thinking and feeling as she looks up at the window? The sky there is barely visible, and the sky we have imagined is filled with all that a sky can be filled with. Am I, in encouraging the children to see the imagined sky, creating an illusion that will be battered by the reality of their urban sky, smoke-filled and intruded upon by buildings that hide much of the daylight? Am I making it more difficult for them to face reality by playing with their invisible sources of seeing, and enabling them to make a fantasized sky that has no resemblance to what they see and experience every day? Am I "teaching" about the sky, or is the sky simply a medium through which I am activating their imaginative powers? Nagging questions, I carry them a good part of my way home.

With no answers, I let the arguments within myself settle down for the night. Within the few remaining classes I have scheduled, surely they will, as children can often do, bring clarification to these issues.

I am strongly inclined to assume that "to imagine" is part of our instinctual abilities. As far as we know, it is most highly developed in human beings, but I am interested in the fact that many species of life other than our own have some form of play. Play is, in part, an illusionary behavior—such as a cat's stalking a piece of string as if it were alive. Play is also an action replete in itself, as when dolphins leap out of the water, monkeys chase each other over tree-tops, or birds fly in circles. And such kinds of play, it seems to me, are primitive forms of the overall instinct to imagine.

In our species, we see forms of play/imagining in very young children—in infants, for example, when they delight at the return of an invisible object or person in the game of peek-a-boo. This play/imagining is not taught to children, but it emerges instinctually and seems to be part of the apparatus with which they begin to savor and understand the nature of their own beings.

When I walk into the room the following week, the children are busy playing. Ms. Golden has given them some free time to go over to the block corner or to the sink with plastic cups, or to the cardboard box which has been converted into an imaginary house. Small groups engage in one thing or another, and the whole room feels like a new morning. Since I have no reason to stop the morning's wakefulness, I tiptoe, with Ms. Golden's permission, from group to group. Even though the children know me—and know our "secret" of the sky—they do not interrupt their play, but invite me to play with them, to kneel down to see what is going on in the shadows of the wooden blocks. I am handed a cup of water at the sink, and I take part in the goodnight talk of a doll put to sleep in the cardboard box.

The classroom is by no means quiet, yet it seems subdued by the intensity of children's concentration. Nothing is being taught to them, yet they are listening, attentive to every detail of their inventing. The cluster of children at the sink is pouring water from one cup to another, and they talk about how much to fill the cup, how quickly to turn the faucet, when to empty the cups with the water. Occasionally they disagree, but only on particulars—about when and how the water should be filled and emptied.

All the while, the water splashes in the sink, its sounds invigorating their talking, washing the patter of their suggestions with reminders that there is work to be done. The supply of water must be kept moving, kept flowing, kept steadily increasing. Why? Because we, the managers of the water, have to make sure the water is doing what it's supposed to do, going and going, filling and emptying, again going and going. They assume the responsibility of being the song of the water itself, a task they have brought into being without adult intentions of teaching them what to do. They revel in their task, each child cooperating with the others to make the water move as it is intended to move.

And the sky today? Maybe we should let the children play, and bring the sky to their play. Let it be the outer shell of their playing, the tent they can play under, the dome of their thoughts where they can see other's thoughts at play. I speak to Ms. Golden about this idea. She says simply, "Why not…"

What I have proposed is more difficult than I initially assumed. To interject my agenda onto what the children are already involved in seems unfair. Perhaps I should let play take its own route, and somewhere along the way, "the sky" will naturally become a part of the unfolding drama. With caution, I go to the group of children in the cardboard house. They greet me, and invite me in once again, and ask if I want to play with them.

"I'd love to," I say. Then, somewhat sheepishly, I add, "And do you mind if I bring the sky along?" Without thinking much about it, they say, simply, "Sure…"

I groan as I get my legs straightened out, and sit with the children. They continue to talk about the life of those inside the house, and Laurie gives me a piece of tattered cloth to clean the wooden block (exported from the block corner with much skill, I assume) which was to be the bed where "you can sleep tonight." She goes on to ask if I am hungry, because they—Laurie, Michele, and Vladimir—are going to start making dinner.

"I'm always hungry…" I whisper back, and the three children take assorted plastic spoons, forks, and paper plates saved by Ms. Golden from various uneaten luncheons. With the bustle of expert preparation, they make a delicious dinner of imagined pizza, sodas, and candy bars.

Dinner is served with much pomp and circumstance. Some torn pieces of paper from the wastepaper basket serve as napkins. I can't refuse anything; and I guess because I ate so much, I begin to get tired quickly. I ask to be excused so I can go to bed. I am soon joined by the children, who want to know if I would like to have a story read to me.

"I'd love that," I say, and I volunteer to give the children small pieces of paper to make storybooks. They accept, and begin to draw. Michele draws stars with legs and arms, and Vladimir starts to make a rainbow. As for Laurie, she is just too busy cleaning the kitchen, and says she will see us later on. In the meantime, Michele and Vladimir fold their pieces of paper as we had done last week, and wait for me to take down their story in their books. Michele rests her arm on mine, and says, quite confidently: "Once upon a time the stars got cold. They put on coats."

"Is that your whole story?" I ask. She thinks for a moment, and then nods. Taking her new book with her picture and her story, she runs off to Ms. Golden to show what she has done.

Vladimir is drawing his rainbow in great detail, and I ask if he would like to tell me his story while he is drawing. "OK," he responds, and with thoughtful pauses, as if the words are opening a door and he is entering a place he has never seen before, he quietly says, "The rainbow...flew...on to earth...and it glows... in my house."

When he finishes talking to me, he goes on making his rainbow; and I wonder where this child, with his curly hair, has found that beautiful word, "glows." It is not a word that one associates with a six-year-old; but here it is, said with the melody it deserves. Who can say why children gravitate to certain words, and how these words become special to them, savored as unique crystals through which entire worlds are reflected?

By this time, my goodnight stories become scattered among the other distractions the children's play eventually takes, and I have to content myself with going to sleep with the satisfaction that I have not only heard two wonderful stories but have witnessed how the sky has entered into the household play. I get up from the cardboard box and visit the other groups. While not everyone has merged our sky adventures with their play of the moment, I hear enough sky-talk to feel that our dome is in place. Our sky is now part of our playing, and we are the imaginers who keep it there.

Our most primary learning is made up of a union of "images" and "sensations" which becomes the personal and unique way we perceive the world. Play of the world within us is the beginning of our instinct to give meaning and structure to experience. Children live their lives by playing, both inwardly and outwardly, fitting image into image until there is a reciprocal feeling between themselves and what the world is about outside.

Because of the intensity of this kind of learning, we can equate it with a kind of poetic knowledge in which our experience is fused with the wonder and awe we experience when we encounter something new, and our awareness and attention is very much present to us—so present that little distinction can be made between ourselves and the object of our awe. Such acuteness of feeling and thought is often what we know as poetry. And this poetic awareness is a part of the development of every child's consciousness. Perhaps it is consciousness itself...

My final two visits with this thoroughly alive class have as much to do with ending as they do with seeing how a process has begun and will continue after I have left the room. The children are delighted to see me arrive and work with them; but, from a larger perspective, they have come to believe that their imagining and their playing are acceptable ways of knowing. What becomes clear is how little effort it takes to bring us back into our sky. If I inquire what the sky may have felt these last few days, I am besieged with answers about the day the sky got sick, the day the stars were unhappy because nobody came to see them, or how yesterday the clouds were making fun of the sun. It seems we are never at a loss for ideas; and we spin marvelous stories, told spontaneously, from the simplest of possibilities.

Because we have arrived at a point where belief and acting on our belief are so strong, Ms. Golden and I decide to devote our last sessions together with the children by dancing, singing, and dramatizing the sky we have internalized. We make up a greeting song to sing to the sky, up and down. We dance, sometimes as the clouds, sometimes as the moon skipping around the sun, sometimes as the rainbow carrying the whole sky to another day. We make up little dramas about the sun's birthday, and how the sky wants to get bigger, and why the moon wants to hang from the night. We share the stories by the children we have put in our "sky box," a rescued shoe box that we put on a table near the window so it can have plenty of daylight.

Throughout, the "noise" that greeted me the first day never diminishes. By now such noise is the constant chatter of minds eager to become the sky they have envisioned, to revel in the thoughts they have brought into existence. It is the hum of those who have seen the sky and know that this too is where they live—and that they are happy to be here. It is Cheneuqua, dancing as a cloud, her round and vibrant face radiating what it feels like when you can let go of who you think you are and become someone else. It is also Cheneuqua spinning around and around as her dizzy cloud who, when I ask the children to stand still and tell us what they felt like being their cloud or their sun or their moon, says, "When I pluck you, little cloud, you are a strawberry to me…" We all smile. And Cheneuqua, sensing our pleasure, smiles back, and her giddy legs spin quickly around a few more times and then she tumbles to the floor and begins to laugh. A laugh, yes, a noise, which somehow glues the world together.

A poetics, where language and the friction of clouds—
collide.

All education is put on hold—when a child looks up,
trying to read the words the sky is saying.

Make the sky fit into a child's hand—and wait for rain.

We yearn for something more than ourselves—to form,
somehow, an intimacy with the world.

What of the child whose exuberance continues to
dance?

Delight is a knowing, too.

A Summer Night:
Remembering Our Childhood
Learnings

The unknown does not crush the void. It dazzles it.

—Edmund Jabes

NOT LONG AGO, a friend and I were trying to remember instances of learning in elementary school. Both of us searched our memories for specific examples of reading a book, solving a math problem, being a part of a discussion, discovering a fact—anything that would place us back in one of the seats we occupied for the first five or six years of our schooling. We did remember being punished—mostly for talking out of turn—and being made, as I was, to sit on the girls' side of the room, or as my friend recalled, being exiled to a small wooden stool for the whole day. But actual examples of learning were simply not accessible to us, at least the kind of learning that was supposed to happen according to what we were being taught.

As I think about my early schooling, I have a vivid recollection of the comfort of daydreaming. I remember the pleasure of "drifting off"—and then of painfully hearing the sharp rebuke of one of my teachers telling me to "pay attention." I can also see the sliding walls on metal tracks of my 5th grade classroom, which could be moved to reveal another classroom on the other side, or the tall unwashed windows that looked down with constantly shifting patterns of light.

It fascinates me that so much memory of childhood learning is not about how we learned, or even what we learned, but what was to be significant and meaningful to us within our growing consciousness. At some vanishing point of memory we remember the small details of particular experiences—the damp smell of the staircase, the way a certain teacher dressed, the sounds of our pencils when we put them inside our wooden desks. But if you ask me the precise feelings and thoughts I had in those many hours and days when I was learning how to read or write or multiply, I admit that I cannot remember much.

Even before going to school, do we have, for instance, any memories of our learning to walk? Certainly shadows are there—as I think back to how I viscerally became a part of my own children's determined efforts to crawl, stand up, and miraculously take their first step forward. But like the memory of my earliest learnings, a finely etched memory of this accomplishment, seems to have receded into a forgotten corner of my mind.

It is dispiriting to realize how much of the inward genius of childhood learning disappears with age, and that it is only with prompting that we are able to catch a glimpse of the marvel of our first years. To counter this loss, I have tried to be on the lookout for the "promptings" as they come to life in the poetry, stories, and artwork of children—or in everyday gestures of playing, talking, and simply being themselves.

One such prompting happened many years ago when my three-year-old son brought a friend, Joshua, home for lunch after nursery school. While my son came quickly into our apartment, ready to eat, Joshua lingered at the door. I noticed he was holding tightly onto a long piece of string that touched the floor. When we finally persuaded him to come inside, he and the string came through the door together. From room to room, wherever he went, Joshua kept dragging the string behind him. When his mother came a few hours later to take him home, my last sight of Joshua was of him quietly walking down the hallway to the elevator with his piece of string still following him.

For over thirty years this picture of Joshua has stayed with me. What has intrigued me is the drama being played out by Joshua—a drama about his desire to hold onto the reality of what that piece of string was, and, at the same time, to keep in view all that he imagined of the invisible at the end of it. He was doing what we all did in our childhoods as we learned to walk or speak or read: He was making visible, through his imagination, the "known" and the "unknown," and using the seemingly opposite qualities as a source of his learning. In the brilliance of childhood playfulness, the string had become his teacher, and he its avid learner.

When I first began working with children, encouraging them to respond to the poetic in themselves, I would sometimes, inspired in part by Joshua's string, come into their classroom with a small empty cardboard box. I wanted children to feel safe around the mysteries and beauty of the "unknown," as well as to continue trusting their ability to play with many transformative elements of the "unknown" itself. In notes I took at the time, after a particular session I had had with a group of younger children, I wrote the following:

Of course nothing is something! It must be a quantity, which if we respond to it, must be something. I am reminded of this when the children are given a sealed box and are asked what they think is inside. "Elephants," they reply, "and dinosaurs, and snakes and air and you're just kidding us, there's nothing inside."

"But," I say, "isn't there anything we can do with nothing?"

So we open a side of the box and let our hands dip inside and take just a little "nothing" and hold it in our closed fists.

I ask them: "What's inside your hands?"

Whispering, they answer: "Heat and darkness and air and nothing."

I then say: "OK, throw a little bit of what is in your hands up into the sky."

And each child, including those most determined to hold on to "nothing," throws away a part of what was in their hands, making sure, at my request, to keep just a little, for later on, curled up in their fists.

Thinking of the children again makes clear for me our need to believe—our need to see in the vastness of the invisible, of the "nothings," multiplying seeds of possibility and aliveness. I am reminded of a summer night when I was eleven, walking with a friend in an open field. Both of us simultaneously noticed how dark it was, and how far away the stars were. We tried talking, but our words seemed too small and fragile against such a large sky. So we simply stood there—without saying anything.

For those brief moments we experienced something neither of us could fully understand. Perhaps we were beginning to feel the profound depth of the world—and of the universe that held us. Or perhaps we were experiencing the magic of the unexplained as it moves towards us, not as facts, but as dimensions of being we had begun to become aware of. Certainly, whatever kept us silent had become a way of learning, a form of knowing that had little to do with what we had been taught in school. We were acknowledging, if only unconsciously, that we were, as separate individuals, many learners in one. And that within our learning, there was another kind of learning we retained and used to feed and nurture the solitary part of ourselves.

Reflecting a few years ago with a group of middle school students about our imaginations, I recalled that one of the students, Dita, had written in her notebook: "Inside my imagination there is a whole new universe."

Reading her sentence now, I try to remember how important were the imaginings of my own childhood. How vital were the inward learnings we kept to ourselves, the smallest details of days and hours and events we stored away to remember later. How crucial was the information we gathered—whether through our growing bodies or the ever absorbing sweep of our senses— which revealed the unique worlds each of us was becoming.

I am unable to recall the exact day of my learning how to spell "house," or how to add 3 plus 3 to equal 6, or what to do when a sentence ends. In the meantime, I clearly remember Joshua's string, the children taking "something" and "nothing" from an empty box, and my own feelings on that summer night when I too was beginning to realize there was a universe, one that is new—and whole—and very real, inside of me. A universe brought together by the stunning and natural gifts of being able to learn to walk, to speak, to make a thought, to unfold a dream, and through remembering to hold an instant of timelessness in our imagining.

Poetic time: the restoration of a time we had known before.

We don't memorize the world: we remember only its particulars.

Teaching—as partially teasing out the invisible, hidden life of the unknown.

What is imagining—but becoming aware of what has been imagined as well—the multitude of a single flower's minuteness.

What is the oldest question? In turn, what is *our* oldest question—the one we were born with?

I Made It By Myself

AS YOUNG CHILDREN, we became conscious of our hands in infancy, when we watched them travel in front of our faces or studied them in the waters of a bath—our fingers floating and causing patterns—or later in school, when we tried to glue with sticky fingers one piece of paper to another. The sensation is still clear: Our hands and fingers were alive and wondrously moved and changed things.

For myself, I experienced a major discovery when I first learned that the solid white ivory keys of the piano made tantalizing sounds when my fingers (and sometimes my rounded fist) banged them. My intoxication with the sounds was endless. I soon found out that my fingers and hands were not isolated extensions of my body, and that, because the sounds were a language, they could speak my feelings. For a long time, playing the piano was my most serious childhood task.

Years later, watching very young children in a classroom, I marveled at how they grasped their pencils and with the same determination I had at the piano, wrote the letters of a word onto their pieces of paper. They were totally absorbed in the new shapes they were making. I was equally captivated when the same children moved to a corner of their classroom and assembled and disassembled wooden blocks with an intensity of builders making something unique.

It is difficult not to wonder where this desire to create was born. How did it manifest itself in these children with such seriousness, spontaneity, and ease? What force in children needs to master the materials they work with so these materials take on a character they did not initially have?

I think of the mounds of mud and sand that have been carefully molded by children—and I remember my own feelings, as a child at the beach. With time set on its side, I busily occupied myself digging a hole in the sand. Gathering layers of sand to protect the hole, and cutting a small entrance, I waited for a wave to creep in. Soon a small river was seeping slowly into the hole. I carefully fixed the entrance so the water flowed more easily, completely absorbed in the details. My world had shape and function: I was totally responsible for what I could make the sand do. I played, not knowing the outcome except in the way my satisfactions were guiding me toward something more to be revealed.

Our impulse to play—at first with our tiny fingers in the air and in water, and then later on with fistfuls of sand—has everything to do with our desire to create. None of us, at an early age, knows the meaning of art or calls herself an artist. Our concern is the material in front of us, its textures, shapes, and smells inviting us to discover what is there. And from images and forms from our exploring comes yet another dimension: what we perceive of as our world. We make things in play from the simplest elements, crisscrossing twigs to make a house or wrapping cloth around a popsicle stick to make a doll, and the practical usefulness of these things is contained within play. Our craft is our play—and when we play, we partake of a knowledge that only the imagination knows when fully engaged: a knowledge when the object of play and our imaginative life are seamlessly merged.

When children create through their play, they receive their

first hint of what creating can mean to them. Their concern is not to make an object, as the adult craftsman does, with the disciplined care of practicing an art. To a child, the pleasure derived from making something, simply to see what paint or clay, a piece of cloth or a twig, can do, is reason enough to continue one's playful investigations.

The desire for play is an instinctive human attempt to uncover what happens only when we play. If we couldn't experiment with a paintbrush, as very young children do, to see what glorious splotches of color and rhythmical curves and circles appear on the paper, then we would be imprisoned in the monotone surfaces of a one-dimensional experience. Play is the great discoverer, and its discoveries are the frontiers and landscapes of our imagining mind. While our hands play, the inner realms of our imaginations grow. We literally learn to see through playing and imagining, a world not only in front of us, but a deeper world suggested by the dance of our imagining self. Listen to this six-year-old child talking about a picture she has painted:

> I have painted some tulips. I have painted them red, yellow, black, a tiny bit of white and a green stalk, and a white pistil, and yellow stamens, yellow and red petals, and black pollen. And there is a tiny bit of red on the end of each petal, and it looks like bubbles, and it feels like some satin, and it looks like a rainbow, and the petals look like hearts.

The child's sensory world has come into being—and bubbles and satin and hearts and a rainbow are quietly made a part of her experience of tulips. The possibilities of paint were brought to life by her hand, but it was the full sense of play that allowed the child to enlarge her image of the tulip. In effect, when our hand

and our imagining mind are mutually at play, we have what is our first attempt to craft our creating. No longer are we spontaneously reacting to materials; we are attempting to change them into what we imagine them to be. How this process, as we grow in years, ultimately tantalizes us, is how some of us decide to spend our time carving, editing, and changing clay, wood, colors, gestures, sounds, and images into what the eye of the imagining self perceives them to be. The adult artist is still the child, happiest (and most curious and anxious) when the materials of our craft are awaiting metamorphosis into meaning and expression. But it is in the actual creating—in the play of thoughts and ideas and elements of our craft—that the satisfaction we had as children is closest to us—when we were keenly aware that our hands and the things they could make and do were an enchantment we could not be without.

The reverential spell of quiet that came upon us as children when we were engrossed in making something was a meeting with what we were making. To be absorbed was not often encouraged, for we were thought to be doing something that had little to do with learning. In retrospect, it was the creation of a story, a poem, a toy boat, or a building made of blocks that we remember now. We remember them because what we were at that moment was engaged in these initial attempts to fashion ourselves and our world.

A few years ago I spoke with children in the first grade who had never been given the opportunity to make this astonishing discovery of themselves. We were speaking about trees, and since there were no trees in the classroom, I asked them to imagine a tree. I encouraged them to feel the bark of the tree, to watch its leaves moving in the wind, and to hear what the tree's roots might sound like drinking the moisture in the ground. How excited the children became when they realized their imagining self—now allowed to play—could picture their own special tree. How eager they were to share their trees with one another. So with paper and crayons they quickly drew pictures of the trees they saw. The reverential spell I spoke of settled over the classroom as each child moved his or her hands, feeling the evolving trees taking shape. When they were finished, each was proud of having created something real and personal. When we asked the children to share their trees with one another, one of them said:

> I made a tree with
> a lot of colors.
> It is just beginning.
> It is very small.

And another child said:

> The roots said how they liked
> how I drawed them. They feel warm and
> they are cousins and brothers and Daddies and
> Mommies. Terrific.

And finally one child, beaming all over, said:

> This is my tree.
> I made it by myself.

Who would have believed that the small and clasping infant hand we once held in front of us would someday, like all human hands, hold a pencil or a paintbrush, turn clay over, or press guitar strings and piano keys—speak them as a gesture in space or let them be touched and moved by what we are saying? Who could have foreseen the joy when these same hands made something, changed something, or brought something into being—joy because we found that our play was asking us to take the smallest of things—a pebble, a string, a clump of dirt—and see what we could do with it?

We played and became artisans of play. And, if we are patient, our play will continually instruct us throughout our lives, telling what we are able to express and create of our lives—still playing.

Testing the unknown—coming up with indecipherable scribbles, a few scratches on the surfaces of thought.

The striving of the human voice—human gesture—to be noticed—to be heard like frogs on the first warm spring night.

Perhaps schooling should be an investment in enchantment, in the wisdom of awe, which will redouble, year after year.

Why are we so impatient to move ahead? For a portion of the day—move sideways, backwards and inside what has no future yet remains significant because of the effort and pleasure it takes to get there.

Becoming a World: Children and Their Poetic Intelligence

SOMETIMES, WHEN I'M OUTSIDE my daughter's elementary school, waiting to take her home, I'm fascinated by the vibrant outpouring of children as they leave the school building. When they finally have the school doors behind them, the great squirming, running and yelling—the sheer letting go of energy that spills out on to the street—always makes me think about the inevitable power of childhood to exert itself.

Yet this daily school ritual also reminds me of another form of childhood exuberance that exerts itself when we listen and watch for it. It's a very different kind of energy though—one that for many children is often quiet and personal. One that seeks intimacy and is often hidden from view. And one, because of its intense blending of thought and feeling, that does not always fit easily into any particular category of intelligence or knowledge.

Both as a parent and a teacher, I have tried to find a way of explaining this way of knowing. It now seems to me that it is basically a poetic exuberance, an intuitive energy that children have without always being able to acknowledge its existence or find a means of expressing.

Given the pressures on children in schools to factualize the world, to maintain a homogenized standard of thought, a poetic way of perceiving experience is simply ignored as an indulgence. There is, in the increasingly test-driven curriculum, little time for it. Still, I have found in my work with children that if we do pay attention to this poetic ability there is a dramatic shift in children's sense of themselves and their desire to learn. By affirming their poetic ability we open up a natural instinct in children to bring the outer world into the inner world of themselves—to link the phenomena of the world, in all its complexity, to the phenomena of one's self.

When I first began teaching, I was made aware of this process when I asked a group of nine-year-old children to become the grass and to dramatize, with spontaneous movement, its nature. Midway through their improvisations I gave out a small piece of paper so they could write down thoughts—as grass. Wayne wrote, "I am a living thing"; Amy wrote, "A drop of green animal"; and Jackie wrote, "I am grass. I grow just like you grow." In the simplicity of their responses was our inherent human gift, through our thought, to reach beyond ourselves to another form of life, to become what we are not and discover, in return, the connectiveness of our lives to other lives.

Let me say at this point that, in the traditional definition of poetry, we were not writing poems—but *becoming*, in effect, the poetry of existence itself. By becoming playful, we allow ourselves to enter into the very fibers, as Wayne reminded us, of "a living thing."

From the start I assumed that this "play" in all its permutations in childhood, was a form of thinking and doing—and most importantly, intelligence. But what kind of intelligence? It is certainly not the general intelligence tested in schools for decades.

Nor does it seem exactly like any of the eight specific intelligences proposed by Howard Gardner. Rather, it is an intelligence that probes ideas, feelings, and the essence of objects. It is an intelligence, brilliantly exploited by young children, that has no fear in examining with hands and feet, or lips and tongue, whatever our bodies can immerse themselves in, in order to get at the pleasure and meaning of *why*, both inside and out, something *is*. In poetic terms, it is a way to discover the unknown without flinching from it, to be curious about the mysterious underpinnings that encircle the world we wish to know.

The French poet, Francis Ponge, in his book *The Voice of Things*, declares that the function of poetry is to "nourish the spirit of man by giving him the cosmos to suckle". And this poetic expressiveness, I am maintaining, begins as an instinctive act of play and imagination. It is an act that, like any other intelligence, has to do with survival, a capacity to learn from and use our experience.

Many years ago in New Zealand I came across a piece of dictated writing by a five-year-old child who attended a one-room school, where the head teacher would, every so often during the school day, invite the children to go outside, lie on their backs, and look up at the sky. From this supine view, this particular five-year-old said:

> I hop
> The shadow hops too
> I lie and think about the sun
> And my shadow thinks about me

Once again the directness and simplicity of thought might distract us from the poetic axis upon which this child pivots its deeper understanding. This thinking is also about play and the child's ever-shifting playful attention to all the players: the shadow, the sun, my shadow, and "me." But, as play frequently does, all the players are directly related to each other, with the end result being a profound observation from this child of a universe in which all things are interactively connected.

The naturalist in the child often grows from its play; for playfulness allows the naturalist to interpret, imaginatively, the world's aliveness. I am quite convinced that one purpose of a child's imagination is to break down the artificial boundaries of human thought so as to move effortlessly between different qualities of being. The child's playful imagination feels no dishonor or shame to inhabit the mind of a flower, a butterfly, and a stone as much as its own mind. By doing so, the child gains a perspective, a footing not unlike that of the mythic singers of indigenous cultures, and the vast poetic traditions of cultures throughout human history. Recently, a nine-year-old child in one class, speaking of himself, said: "My imagination is part bird—and part wildflowers." This was from a child on the Lower East Side of Manhattan, whose usual sightings from his classroom windows are the buildings of a highly urbanized metropolis.

What are we to make of this statement except to consider the possibility that far below the surface of our everyday thinking another means of knowing exists—a kind of knowing that began far back in the biological history of our thought. Perhaps Thoreau was correct to ask: "Shall I not have intelligence with the earth? Am I not partly leaves and vegetable mould myself?" Or Edith Cobb, who states in her book *The Ecology of Imagination in Childhood*: "As man, woman or child, we are living portions of the vast historical continuum that is nature." Or recently, ten-year-old Man Shan who told me: "I see a lot of nature when I can play."

Thus exuberance is what we reveal when our play is our poetry. When our poetic intelligence, with its confluence of thought and feeling, brings us back to our earlier evolutionary past where we felt a kinship with all life forms. It is the same intelligence that allows a nine-year-old urban child, Qweshon, to write: "I think the trees have a conversation of nature." Angie, another child in the same school wrote: "My tree likes to look at stars—and its leaves make the wind change colors. My tree likes to give life to dead things." It is an intelligence that has the capacity to widen our collective and individual understandings because, as both player and imaginer, the child and we become active participants in the poetry of ourselves and of others—both human and non-human.

How could I doubt this possibility after working a few years ago with a group of seven- and eight-year-old children in a crowded classroom, thinking together about the rainy and stormy weather of the night before. We were wondering about how rain falls, where thunder and lightning come from, and what perhaps the moon might be doing behind the clouds. As we spoke it was obvious we had to take the next step—we had to become the storm. And so I asked: "Who would like to be the moon, the rain, the clouds, the lightning and thunder?" Hands went up everywhere—and off in the corner of the room a small girl, quietly and confidently, went beyond merely *being* the thunder and said: "I want to be *thundered*."

Yes, here again was the poetic intelligence. Not the intelligence of the correct answer, or the right use of language, but an intelligence that takes us, to the primary sense of poetry as a presence, an act of presence within the very thing we are talking about. The late American poet, Cid Corman, echoes this way of thinking when he writes:

> Follow
> the stream:
> Dont go—
> but be
> going.

Within every child I suspect is the same desire to know the stream not only as a subject matter, but also as its moving waters, to be the poetry of the thing itself, whether it happens to be the grass, the sun, a tree, or thunder. And by becoming this poetry, each of us, child and adult alike, have the possibility of becoming ever closer to the very forces, the exuberance, and energy that we share with the intelligence that is nature itself.

> The wind is air that moves to find
> more air. Wind wants to create by
> pictures. Wind is a making of the
> world.
>
> *—Camille, age 11*

Letting our everyday intelligence go mute: to feel the intelligence of what surrounds us.

Take a tree, a flower, a blade of grass—and study their stillness. Become their stillness; aware only of the air your imagining begins in.

There is something in our learning—which begins and ends—without words.

Often the poetic must remain our most quiet, unspoken experience—a healing silence from the cacophony of explanations.

The point is *not* to teach—but to evoke, to stir our desire to believe differently.

Invent as many dawns as you can.

The Thousand Fragments

A FEW WEEKS AGO, going through some old books of mine, I found this short poem by the contemporary Greek poet George Seferis:

> How can you gather together
> the thousand fragments
> of each person?

Like much poetry, which speaks across time, this poem lingered with me. It became, after a number of days, not just a poem, but a mentor's request. And like an eager student I broke apart the poem's question into other questions. What does it mean "to gather," to bring "together"? What are "the thousand fragments" in each of us? Are they our inarticulate, sometimes invisible thoughts, the many fleeting images of experience we grasp and hold onto only occasionally?

Sitting alone for a while, I felt that the world that I am does seem fragmentary, as if the ever-pulsating sensory antennae of my mind never stop creating the minute and fragile thoughts that are what I know and understand as my world. Yet to make sense of the fragments—let alone gather them—isn't this what my learning, our learning, is about? Isn't this what we, as human life, have been attempting to do from the time that we—as individuals and as a species—spoke our very first words? Isn't this what our first drawings and gestures, our first songs and stories, were inventing: a way to describe, a way of knowing who we are within ourselves and in the world around us?

Just this year when I was working with a group of five-year-olds, one of the children raised his hand and, in a marvel of childhood juxtapositions, excitedly asked, "Can I tell you a question?" Though for a moment I was startled by his request, I soon realized that he had, perhaps unbeknown to himself, repositioned questioning into the primary place it is, and must be, in our learning. Instead of telling a story—he was about "to tell" a question. There it was, hovering over us, glowing in all its epic possibilities and drama.

I later shared his question with a group of teachers in a workshop I was giving on the poetic life of childhood, and they immediately recognized what the five-year-old had brought to *their* own thinking. Like leaves of tea settling into the warm water, their response had as much to do with a new respect for their own childhood as it did with the subtlety of the child's thought. He reminded us not only of our own beginnings as children but also of the ways in which our initial expressions to understand the fragments and thoughts within us are part of an older lineage linking us to the earliest attempts of human consciousness to express itself.

Years ago, in response to an arts project entitled "Earth Makers in the Earth Garden" (which I was directing in a junior high school in New York City), Dawn, one of the sixth graders in the project, wrote:

> My father taught me how to make flowers:
> (1) How deep to dig.
> (2) How much dirt to cover the seed.
> (3) How to move your hand to make it grow.
> (4) How long to wait.

The magic is just the way your hands move.

Like the child asking me if he could "tell" a question, here was another child, an eleven-year-old, expressing not only the mystery of how things grow but the unfolding mystery of how thoughts, and especially imaginations, are brought into being. The magic, as she suggests, is in the hands, in the way we let our imaginations move over the dwelling place of growing.

Once again we are a participant in the ageless lineage of human expression. A father tells his daughter how to make flowers grow, she tells me—and I share her thoughts with you. And as I write these lines I realize how much the act of writing has to do with my desire, as a teacher, writer, and parent, to bring the expressiveness, and our capacity to imagine, into the conversation with ourselves and each other.

I believe that in all of us there is a gathering instinct echoing back to the hunting and gathering skills of our earliest human ancestors. The same ability *to gather* is crucial in our making sense of "the thousand fragments," which constitute our solitude. Not a solitude that might be seen as idle and unresponsive, but one, with the help of *gathering* skills, that constantly sifts and arranges the vast network of our thoughts and feelings. A solitude that becomes consciousness and our most convincing sense of being alive.

If we look closely at ourselves we can see how the solitary task of *gathering* began in childhood, and continues throughout our lives. It is one of the tasks from which we learn to teach ourselves—and is as vital to us as is our need to be taught by others. And like the excited five-year-old, we too cannot resist "telling" our questions—forever exploring the shapes and designs, the intricate mosaics, of who we are. Scattered over the course of human evolution, the records of the inward explorations surface abundantly: in our stories and poetry, our dance and drama, our art and music—in the endless symbols and metaphors we have invented to explain ourselves and the world we experience.

With much contemporary education stifling the solitary learning—asking of children only questions that require quantifiable answers—we lose our original knowledge. We are made to forget the essential relationship between thinking and feeling, and the life forces existing throughout the natural world. We abandon the human ability to deepen our human awareness and perceptions in the same way a tree deepens and spreads its roots. We sacrifice our gift for wonder, and our natural awe for the unknown, by defining the imagination as something—not true.

Given these losses, we need, as adults, to advocate for the role of solitary learning—in ourselves and in children. We need to pay closer attention to the imagination as a source of understanding—and to listen more acutely to the centrality of imaginative thought and play in children—and to its implication for our adult lives. We need to regain the poetry of learning, the surprise and delight, the magic and mystery that brought each initially to become learners. We must acknowledge those "thousand fragments" in ourselves as the same fragments that constitute the richness and complexity, the endless cycle of living and dying, found throughout nature. Such an acknowledgement will enable us to continue to clarify and bring meaning to the world and ourselves.

It was a long dry winter in the East this year—a year, 2001, marked by numbing tragedy and fear. When spring finally came and the rains began to fall, the sudden greening, the hypnotic smells of a new freshness, were everywhere. It felt to me, as our inward worlds sometimes feel—a resurgence of aliveness, of thoughts brought into a new alignment, of being able to find a balance again within the ever-present dualities and contradictions of existence. It seemed, as these words of the 12th century Chinese poet Yang Wan-li convey—a world that, even as we age, never ceases asking to be understood. A world in which the many fragments of our thoughts and feelings can come together, perhaps as a luminous moment we experience in ourselves and, over time, we can bring to others.

Night Rain at Guang-Kou

The river is clear and calm;
    a fast rain falls in the gorge.
At midnight the cold, splashing sound begins,
like thousands of pearls spilling onto a glass plate,
each drop penetrating the bone.
In my dream I scratch my head and get up to listen,
I listen and listen, until the dawn.
All my life I have heard rain,
    and I am an old man;
but now for the first time I understand
    the sound of spring rain
        on the river at night.

—*Yang Wan-li*

To get into the mind of a question—become the smallest of thoughts, not yet imagined.

The spine of thought is the imagination.

The part of us—stretching our necks to see over the wild grass—the part that will not, does not want to be explained.

We are still ancient questions learning to ask.

On the one hand—the brutality of the imagination—to destroy. On the other—the compassion of the imagination—to defend what is alive.

The Other Side of Knowing:
Keeping Alive the Magic
of Imaginative Thought

SITTING ON A CITY BUS the other day, I overheard a little boy, perhaps four or five years old, who, as he was looking out the window, asked his mother, "When is it going to rain?" She shrugged her shoulders—and he, undeterred, quietly answered: "The clouds will know."

There, to my delight, in the briefest of conversations, was what we as teachers often attempt to make happen, but given the formal and historic relationship between ourselves and those we teach, we find difficult to bring about. The mother illustrated how, when we don't know an answer, we can simply step back and let the child, learned in his or her own ways of knowing, answer for us.

But there was something else that caught my attention. Here, in the maddening rush and noise of the city, the child, without any self-consciousness, uncovered an element of the poetic magic that exists in natural phenomena. It is a poetic magic that has everything to do with how a young child animates the world, and sees life in everything that exists outside of herself. It's a perception of the living, dynamic qualities in the universe that hovers between scientific accuracy and the excitement and subtleties of simple awe—such as the poem that my daughter Sarah, when she was five, asked me one morning to write down for her:

> The sun
> brightens
> out
>
> in one
> more
>
> today.

At the other end of the solar spectrum, Josh, also five years old, saying:

> I know how daytime changes to nighttime.
> Daytime melts.

Such perceptions are spontaneous expressions of the "magic" of daylight—the "brightening" and "melting" all of us can attest to in the unfiltered immediacy of our perceptions. Or as Thoreau said, "The question is not what to look at but what you see."

Ever since I began working with children I have tried to make use of this animated quality of thinking. I have tried to understand how it is really at the heart of a child's, and our own, innate capacity to experience the world — along with our desire to give shape and expression to the experience. I can vividly remember as a young child sitting by a stream on a large rock and looking down at the fish swimming beneath the rock. For a moment, I felt as if I was one of the fish—moving gently to the undulating motion of the water, afraid and yet curious, of the shifting currents of light and darkness. It was an instance where the line between myself and what I was looking at had dissolved—and I was a participant in something larger than my own body. It seemed, and still seems, in the most primary sense of being—magical.

Yet this sense of magic has all too often been relegated to early childhood. Throughout much of our later schooling we were taught to see and experience things for what they are. We were made to believe that "nature" is an objective reality—and that clouds and fish are not us—but occurrences and lives that happen outside of us. This disconnect has brought the feeling of isolation that pervades the lives of both children and adults—as they try to find a profounder meaning to their relationship with the natural world.

I keep this in mind when I come into a room and begin speaking with children. This winter, for instance, I sat down with a group of young children at Poets House in New York City and asked them whether they had noticed the snow that had fallen the night before. Some had noticed it; others had not. As we continued talking, it was obvious that the best approach would be to evoke, to bring the children's attention back to the marvel of snowflakes falling. I took a small envelope from a wooden box (where I keep my secrets), and held it high above my head. For a few seconds the children were puzzled by the unopened envelope, my silence, and our waiting. Then, as if the sky had given its permission, I opened the envelope and let fall many, many tiny pieces of torn white paper. Instead of just falling, they floated, one piece of torn paper at a time, down to the floor. I could see that the children were suddenly riveted, in startled belief, as the snow gathered around us.

"Can these snowflakes feel anything?" I asked.

And one of the children replied, "They feel the air."

I asked again, "What does it feel like, what does the air feel like?"

Another child called out, "Rrrrr…hard. If the air is hard, the snowflakes will push it aside."

At that moment in our conversation we had moved to a place where our knowing had been brought a step closer to a child's way of seeing—and both our floating snowflakes and the entranced children had entered a consciousness of their own. It was a consciousness, perhaps, in which each child's imagination held the magic simultaneously of ourselves, the air—and the snowflakes. In poetic terms, it was the "hidden glimmering" that the 17th century Japanese haiku poet, Basho, spoke of when he wrote: "Your poetry issues of its own accord when you and the object have become one—when you have plunged deep enough into the object to see something like a hidden glimmering there." Or as the essayist Annie Dillard observed: "What I call innocence is the spirit's unself-conscious state at any moment of pure devotion to any object. It is a receptiveness and total concentration."

It can be argued that encouraging children to think this way is, in the long run, antithetical to the immediate task of training disciplined minds for the future. It can be seen as a slowing down, an avoidance of what the mind wants eventually to do in order to grasp the complexities of life as we live it now. In some circles this argument has validity — but time and time again I have used a similar approach with teachers of all ages—and have found that quite the opposite is true. That as adults we need to be equally aware as children of the other side of knowing—that we need to reaffirm the link to our inborn ability to perceive the "nature" of things and the myriad phenomena existing within and outside of ourselves. We need to feel the poetry everywhere around us—and what the contemporary poet Robert Bringhurst speaks of when he says: "What poetry knows, or what it strives to know, is the dancing at the heart of being." Or, as the Pygmies in Africa have celebrated in one of their chants:

I throw myself to the left.
I throw myself to the right.
I am the fish
Who glides in the water, who glides
Who twists himself, who leaps.
Everything lives, everything dances, everything sings.

The magic that the child encounters—that it brings to the surface of its thoughts—is, in fact, this "everything." It is a child's intuitive understanding that comes into play when a drop of rain or a snowflake opens out into a deeper and wider knowledge, simply because there, within the rain and the snow, are all the elements of life itself.

The child is, before anyone has taught her to be otherwise, something of the original magician. She takes a little of the *known* and a little of the *unknown* and mixes them in the fertile space of her imagining. What appears and is expressed by the child is another kind of knowledge, another kind of learning, that allows us to discover and understand our sense of being in the world—in a new and, perhaps, magical way.

A rock is a whole world.

—*Cody, age 5*

The tree sees feeling.
And feels as it goes deeper
and deeper.

—*Shuab, age 11*

Finding the rhythms of the unknown, the private music
of our own awareness.

The poetic—as a biological link, a means of thought that
is our relationship, our intimacy with all forms of life.

To speak of the part of us that has not yet been codified.

The cell-life of enchantment—multiplying without us.

We are capable of hearing beyond our ears—a sense of
being that listens for us after we have stopped thinking.

It is we who are the audience—for a tree's silence.

What would happen if we truly threw out all the names
of knowing—and started all over?

Dreaming Into Waters

It takes a lot of dreaming to understand a
stretch of still water.

—Gaston Bachelard

WHEN I WAS A CHILD I liked going out on a lake in a rowboat. I was supposed to be fishing, but the lazy drift of the boat, the endless patterns of small waves, and the flooding sunlight all seemed to hold my attention instead. Even now I feel myself tapping into sensations that seem more visceral than definable, and I ask myself, are such sensations actual knowledge? Are they, in our empirical and fact-saturated culture, worth lingering over? Will they, in the end, matter to anyone except myself?

After many years of trying to help children discover their poetic and imaginative abilities, I am now convinced that such sensations not only are valuable but are one of the foundations of a child's instinctive propensity to daydream. For daydreaming is often triggered when we are brought into contact with the most basic phenomena of life and we become intuitively aware of our primordial past, as it exists in both the visible and invisible elements of the natural world.

How many of us can vividly remember occasions when we stood silently watching the falling snow, a tree moving in the wind, the passage of morning light—and, if only momentarily, letting our minds succumb to something inarticulate in ourselves: something that seemed far removed from our daily existence, yet brought us closer to a memory, a remnant of feeling much older than ourselves. Even though we were fully conscious, our thoughts ebbed and changed as if dreaming, as if we were inside what we were watching.

Not long ago, I happened to look out of my apartment window and saw a girl about five years old step into a puddle. Her mother disapproved and tried to get her to continue walking, but the girl would not leave. Instead she wiggled her yellow-booted feet until the water in the puddle was stirring in all directions. She seemed, despite her mother's pleading, to be perfectly content to be right there, in the middle of the puddle, lost in her delight. While I cannot vouch for what she was thinking, I suspect she was, like most children, perfectly at ease in her watery universe, dreaming happily with its liquidity, its aliveness as water. She was in the most obvious sense playing, but her fleeting moments in the puddle remind me that her playing, her dreaming, was also a part of our larger human endeavor to link, through our imaginative abilities, the action and gestures of nature with the inward movements of our thoughts.

Like this girl, many indigenous cultures have felt the influences of the powerful nature of water. The puddle she stepped in could as easily have been the sacred water holes where various Aboriginal tribes of Australia come into contact with their totemic ancestors who make up their *dreamtime*, their highly complex mythic story of the creation of our world and its universe. Or her puddle could have been one of the pools of water the Plains Indians of North America believed were created from the glowing pieces of a star that crashed onto the earth, out of which a young girl took some "star water" to hang "around the necks of her people, so that everyone could see where everyone else was."

While these understandings are part of deeply-rooted spiritual traditions passed on from one generation to another, they also demonstrate how we attempt to bring meaning and continuity to our experience. Somewhere in us is our need to move away from a purely scientific definition of water, and go to a place where we, like the child in the puddle, do not wish to be separated from the puddle. And this place is where our dreaming, our imagining, comes into play.

I recently completed a collaborative project with an art teacher and a visual artist in a public school in New York City, where I worked with a mixed classroom of first and second graders. Over a period of ten weekly one-hour sessions, we explored the elements of air, water, and light. Our goal was to bring the children to the spaces of imaginative thinking where their conscious dreaming could return the elements to how they were being experienced—on another level of knowing.

On the first day, I brought in an eyedropper filled with tap water. I slowly pinched the head of the eyedropper so that only a small drop of water hung at the bottom. We were all quite breathless—as this tiny fragment of water reflected the room around us, and moved, ever so slightly from the air touching it. As the children stared at its fragile body, I asked them: "If you could go inside this drop of water, what would you see there, what does it feel like, what might the water be feeling?"

There were lots of spontaneous replies—and I realized how little effort it took the children to move, imaginatively, into the interior of the drop of water. After a while I asked if they would like to make a watercolor painting of the drop of water. Paint they did, creating vibrant abstract and impressionistic images. Using their paintings as a guide, I then suggested that they might trans-late the paintings into words. While some needed help in getting their thoughts down, everyone seemed eager to write, to find a quiet corner in the room, where, on their own, they could dream and write about the transparent world they had just entered.

> Water swishes to a beach and goes back.
> It wishes it can walk.
> Little children swim in the water.
> Water feels happy.
> But still it wishes it can walk.
> Sunlight shines on the water, all the time.
>
> *—Olivia*

> When you are on the water
> it feels like you are on the sky.
>
> *—Max*

> Water is soft. It is wet. It can move a lot of ways.
> There are a hundred different waters in your
>   imagination.
> Water is magic.
>
> *—Darrow*

Darrow's insight—that "there are a hundred different wa-ters in your imagination"—brought to mind the Taoist thought of Chuang-tzu, who said, "The sound of the water says what I think." And isn't this way of thinking how we bring ourselves into the framework of natural phenomena; how the "nature" of our imag-ining connects to the "nature" that lies outside of ourselves? Evidence became apparent when we saw the children the following week. During this interim period, with the inspired help of their classroom teacher, they had continued to explore the drop of water now as only an image in their memory—and they reached further into the actual qualities of the dreaming.

> Water dreams about the beach.
> And the water likes to go down on
> the ground.
>
> And rain likes to go on the
> ground too.
>
> *—Justin*

> Water dreams about going in a cup
> and waiting for someone to drink it.
> The water wants the kids to love it.
>
> *—Dylan*

In each piece of writing the children have expressed a way to fuse their observations of water with what we, as humans, are about. This is not false personification or animism. It is the blending of our human impulses and feelings with lives outside of us. It is a recognition of a mutual "livingness" existing everywhere; and it is a knowledge as important as anything we might learn from a textbook. It is, as the philosopher Paul Shepard suggested, recognition of our thought as "an ecological activity, a process" in which "we are recipients as well as actors in a world of Others."

Could my daydreaming in the rowboat have been what all children do in order to come closer to the life within water—and in turn, the life within themselves? Could it have been the other side of knowing, our imaginative knowing, that cannot be taught but only encouraged to come to the surface?

Whatever I might say about these questions, I will leave it to one of the children to sum up what dreaming means.

> My imagination is in a place where there is water and light.
> There is a boat. When you see it, it stops.
> Then you get on it.
>
> —*Isabella*

It is the art of timing—of knowing when to begin—
when to allow the accidents of thought to be the prime
mover.

Reflective learning—making us aware of what we lose
every day, if we don't pay attention.

At the back of the classroom—a table for clouds and
rain and shifting light.

Sustaining the small undercurrent of childhood we
continually look out from.

Surrounded by children, I want to listen—to be
absorbed by their thoughts, to be their dreaming
out loud.

A Flickering Light

BETWEEN GETTING UP in the morning and going to sleep at night, children, everywhere, have a poem—in waiting. Most would not call it poetry, but if you explore the idea, most would admit to a feeling, a way of sensing, different from their ordinary feelings and thinking. If you question further, many children can detect, and even identify, a particular kind of experience that occurred when they were playing or daydreaming, sitting by themselves or talking to someone, where contrary aspects of their world had come together.

I myself remember walking on a country road when I was about ten years old, and becoming acutely aware of the trees and sky around me—and feeling how I, too, was growing and changing with those trees and their sky. It was a short-lived feeling, but as I grew older it became a part of my memory and consciousness, quietly evolving into questions and imaginings. Once on a cold, windy day in a fifth grade classroom in Canada, when I first began working with children, John Harding, one of the students in the class, came up afterwards and shyly handed me a slip of paper. On it he had written, "A poem is a flickering light that has been spotted on a scene that not many of us have seen or heard of before."

Reading John's words again reminds me how many children in his class had never been given the opportunity to hear poetry.

More than that, though, they had never been told of the poetry within themselves. While I had spent part of the time in his class reading poems by adult poets, it wasn't until I began reading poems by other children that they, as a group, began to listen differently. In some transformative way, they seemed to hear as if for the first time, the secretive feelings and thoughts that they had experienced—but now were given permission to reveal.

And yet, the feelings and thoughts beneath the surface of children's everyday life can easily be overlooked. Certainly in a time like ours, when extensive pressure is placed on children to work toward test-proven ideas, the expression of their inner worlds may be put aside as a waste of time. But by doing so we dismiss the origins, and sources, of their imagination. From the first breathlike unwindings of their gestures, drawings, and words, children need to know that their innate desire to connect what they have felt and experienced inwardly, has a deep, lasting relation to what they outwardly express, and often generously share with others.

They also need to be reassured that the desire for expression is embedded within the history of human thought, that as far back in time as when we painted our hands onto cave walls, chanted our songs across open fields, carved our wooden masks, or danced our ancient stories, we were responding to a basic need to complete and form the images within us. Such forming and completing—making visible what is invisible—is as natural and instinctive as our playing, dreaming, walking, and talking.

The 17th century Japanese haiku poet Basho said: "No matter what we may be doing at any given moment, we must not forget that it has a bearing upon our everlasting self, which is poetry." For those working and living with children, the challenge is how to find an entry point to the poetry. Like the varied hues of individual experience, there is no one way to do this. Instead, what initially we must be certain of, is our belief that there exists within every child a profound process of feeling and thinking that enables each of them to bring together an individual synthesis of inward and outward worlds. And, as importantly, we must be convinced that the assembling, the ageless act of imagining, is as crucial to learning as any mandatory subject matter.

The "flickering light," the unique poem in each of us, is one of our oldest, and perhaps most meaningful means of saying who we are, where we are, and what enlivens us. It is a language—one of the many languages we have evolved to communicate the endless variety of human experience. For children, might it not be something of the fullness of being they wish to grasp—in the same way this child penciled on the first page of her empty notebook:

What I want to write about. Everything.

Much of the time we wake up to a vastness—
we instinctively try to make smaller.

What do we see when we are not looking?

We blunt the inarticulate—the unanswered in ourselves.

Are we mostly a secret we haven't found yet?

What, if one day, you wrote a sentence that lingered on
the branches of a tree?

What Trees Know:
Talking with Teachers about the Imagination of Being

WHAT ELSE IS THERE TO SAY: a little girl, perhaps three or four years old, running down a low sloping hill in Central Park, her arms and legs abandoning themselves to the push and pull of gravity, while trailing behind her, exuberant with spring air, the floating sounds of her childish laughter.

What else is there is there to say, when here, in a very small moment, are all the elements of what our aliveness so often is: wordless, almost invisible, yet completely evident and felt. This was an "aliveness" I was trying to convey to a group of New York City classroom teachers recently, teachers who were taking a summer workshop on the identification and understanding of the natural world. Invited to speak about the imagination in learning, I did not want to circumvent the relevance of science within the workshop. Instead, I wanted to move the information they were studying to a different perspective. I sensed that we had to shift our attention to the child running down the hill—to the purely sensuous experience, to a form of knowledge that cannot be measured on a scale of learned abilities.

I asked them what they do on their summer vacations, and

they overwhelmingly mentioned relaxing, taking time off from regular activities. Then, after some probing, they elaborated on how they enjoyed sitting near water, gardening, listening to waves, walking in a forest, watching birds, being quiet. When I moved the conversation to the children they teach, most agreed that what they did during the summer was what the children had no opportunity to do during the school year. What was expected of them as teachers was to teach the known quantities of learning, those fractions of knowledge that can be measured. They pointed out that sitting, walking, listening—or running down a hill—were not subjects with any reliable means of accountability. I concurred, and asked again what kinds of thoughts and feelings they had when they participated, during their summer vacations, in these activities. Slowly, and with some encouragement, they admitted to feeling young again, and aware of being part of something more than this human frame of ours. Some said they were sometimes conversant with a language not only between themselves, but also with the waters nearby, the sand they were playing with, the birds they could hear—even another voice within their own speaking. I suggested that such a language may come from the ability of our imaginations to enter into the things we are watching, listening to, and sitting with. Such imagining is a form of knowing that children, by the indigenous nature of their childhood, use as an active understanding—of being at the heart of their and others' aliveness.

Maybe then, I suggested, trees (which they were studying that day) cannot be identified only by their leaves, or bark, or the shape of their branches, but by their relationship to us personally. Maybe the qualities of a tree's presence—the story it tells in our minds, the sounds it makes in the wind—are the qualities we first knew, as young children.

As we spoke one of the teachers said she often thought about what trees know, what they must have seen or heard as trees. I smiled to myself because for a number of years now the artist-teachers of The Touchstone Center and I have been exploring a similar question with children we work with. Like the teacher, we have expanded our definition of knowing, of learning, to include all forms of natural life—and in particular the knowledge inherent in trees.

Some children who participated in this Tree of Knowing project shared these thoughts with us.

> My tree knows it's not alone
> My tree feels strong because it has branches.
> The branches are not heavy.
> They are connected to each other
>   and the air and light.
> The tree is never in the dark.
> It always has light inside.
>
> —*La Porsche, 5th/6th grade*

> I think we know what a tree dreams
> because at night we sleep next to a tree
> and it is like two thoughts together.
>
> —*Case, 3rd/4th grade*

I stressed how an innocence prevails—but it is not an innocence we need to give up because it seems useless in the competitive forward motion of schooling. It is an innocence that relies on children's innate ability to become a part of what they see and experience, to believe, through their imagination, that everything is as alive and responsive as they are. It is often children's lack of factual knowledge that allows them to rely on what they know through their senses and imaginations. It is an innocence—an imaginative capacity—that we adults sometimes wish to return to and find ourselves once again experiencing the world in all its *being-ness* and immediacy. In a subtle and precise way, the 17th century Japanese haiku poet Basho captured this kind of innocence when he wrote

> Not knowing
> The name of the tree
> I stood in the flood
> Of its sweet smell.

I have always been fascinated by children's ability to take the simplest of objects—a ball, a stone, a twig, a marble, a feather— and build upon it a multitude of worlds. I have been intrigued by how quickly I can give children a pinch of air I hold between my two fingers—and without much convincing, ask them to smooth its edges, tickle its sides, turn it up so it faces the sky, and carefully put it in the palm of their hand. I am certain now the ability to have confidence with the invisible, as well as to treat the most invisible of elements with awe and respect, is due to the fluidity of their imaginations.

Yes, this might be innocence as well, but it is at the very basis of all our poetic and scientific thought, of a way of thinking that reaches out and integrates disparate ideas and possibilities that emerge from the unknown. It's about what this six-year-old exclaimed: "Oh wow! Air opens. Air can open."

Or what the philosopher Gaston Bachelard observes: "There are moments in childhood when every child is the astonishing being, the being who realizes *the astonishment of being*."

When children are free at play, and not apparently doing anything related to school—this is a time of their aliveness and also their contemplation. When we think of the moments of childhood, when we were really being children, we often remember our questioning. Amidst running, playing, and shouting, for a brief moment, we stopped to look at the ground, and began to wonder why the leaves were going the same way we were going, why they fell, who would be there to catch them, who gave them colors, what they felt, and where they will be when it snows.

A child's questions, certainly, but questions filled with a child's way of asking—balancing the known and the unknown, the imagined and the real. As importantly, we can hesitate and think like children again. We can vacation ourselves in a leaf's world. And what might we call this hesitation—the departure from everything that we are supposed to be doing and taking place around us? Might it simply be the craft of our imaginations, like those of children, to speak through and with the language of our being: the marvel of our imaginative genes to build a bridge between ourselves and the community of all the other living elements that make up our world? Might we once again think like the fourth grader Ashrat, who says,

> The light likes to play with me.
> The light is going all around the world.
> And the other lights are dancing.
> I like those lights so much.
> I love the dancing and the going around the world.

Children may not be fully aware of the impact of their astonishment, playfulness, and imagining on their lives. But I would offer, as I did with the teachers, that in a vital, hidden corner of our imaginations, we have imprinted those seemingly insignificant moments, and these moments sustain us as persons and keep us related to the world. The world's abundant elements—light, air, water, plants, insects, and animals—constitute our collective sense of being, and are far from useless. They are the essential body of the imaginative conversation we must continue if we, and our planet, are to have a viable future.

To be able to seek out the simplest of means in order to play—the strength of what the simple is.

Schooling should not be about "failure"—but about satisfaction—and the accomplishment of meaning.

Andrew, in the sixth grade—and his matter of factness when he said: "I hang my imagination up—so it can get air—so it can fly—because it hasn't done so for over a year."

Does the mind migrate? To where and when?

Carry a stone, a feather and a seashell. If not these, the hand, always naked, will do.

"Mr. Lewis—guess what, I've been keeping this piece of dust for you all weekend."

Dragonfly

I MET A CHILD recently whom I hadn't seen for a long time. He took it upon himself to remind me of things we had done in class together, emphasizing in broad gestures that the imaginary dragonfly we had talked about was still in his pocket—where he had put it just before he left the room on the last day. We began to talk about how the dragonfly was feeling now, where it had flown, and what it might be thinking about all this time. Very little had changed about the dragonfly, which, though tucked away, had not been smothered, even after the intervening years. It was my impression as I talked to this child that this dragonfly was about to fly again.

It is precisely this storage capacity of the child's mind that reveals the power of the imaginative experience as an imprint upon growing thought. The imprint is very much like a significant quotation we hold onto in order to articulate and guide us through a particular human dilemma. For this child, the dragonfly represented any number of human actions and desires, but the fact that it could be retained over a long period without a flaw in detail speaks tellingly of the degree to which the imaginative experience creates its own boundaries of time and manner of reproducing itself. The image of the dragonfly was more than just a dragonfly—perhaps invested in it was the child's own fascination with the translucency of thought; thought weaving in and out of itself in order to reach itself; and thought, like the dragonfly, wonderfully alive and real as it hesitates in mid-air, throbbing in its flight to stand still, and darting elsewhere from that momentary point of stillness.

In a broader sense, it is the child's acceptance of thought as an image; an image befriended and made a companion within the stranger complexities of reality. To the child, the dragonfly lives, not only on an external level, but as an image that can be called upon to narrate, and if need be, to fly next to his own awakening consciousness. To the child, there is no need to forget the dragonfly, for it flies, like himself, a similar course, catching the same sunlight in its vibrancy.

I love dragonflies....but one day
I saw a colorful dragonfly.
It was beautiful and when I put it
in my cage, it flew out.
I let it go home.

—David P., 3rd Grade

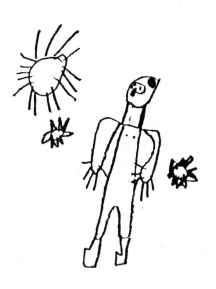

CREDITS

My thanks to the following publications and organizations where these essays and writings were first published:

Encounter: Education for Meaning and Social Thought
Becoming a World: Children and Their Poetic Intelligence
(Vol. 17, Number 4, Winter, 2004)
The Other Side of Knowing: Keeping Alive the Magic of Imaginative Thought (Vol.19, Number 3, Fall, 2006)
Dreaming Into Waters (Vol.18, Number 3, Fall, 2005)
What Trees Know: Talking With Teachers About the Imagination of Being (Vol. 20, Number 3, Fall, 2007)

Paths of Learning
A Summer Night: Remembering Our Childhood Learnings (Summer, 2004)
The Thousand Fragments (Fall, 2002)

New Horizons for Learning
I Made It By Myself (Fall, 2002)

C.A.R.T.S. National Newsletter for City Lore
A Flickering Light (Vol. 5, Spring 2001)

Intersection: Testing a World View, Irish Museum of Modern Art, Spring, 1996 and **Teaching Artist Journal, Winter, 2005** - for previously published *Reflections*

ACKNOWLEDGMENTS

My gratitude to David Appelbaum, publisher of Codhill Press, for his editorial sensitivity and insights—as well as his enthusiasm for bringing this book to a larger audience. And my thanks to the professionalism of Shanti Fader for her proofreading, Heidi Neilson for her design work, and to Carol Inskip for creating an index.

In addition, my appreciation to William Crain, Dee Dickinson, Richard Prystowsky, Eric Booth, Helen O'Donoghue, Amanda Dargan, and Monroe Cohen for their thoughtful editing of these essays and writings in their original form and publication.

And to my children Amanda, Sascha, and Sarah and my grandchildren Benjamin and Daniel, for the pleasures and understandings they have given me, and my wife Carol, who encouraged, listened and made real the necessity of it all—my delight and love.

NOTES

Becoming a World

Cobb, Edith. 1977. *The Ecology of Imagination in Childhood*. New York: Columbia University Press, pp. 100-101.

Corman, Cid. 1983. *Aegis: Selected Poems, 1970-1980*. Station Hill, p. 99

Gardner, Howard. 1983. *Frames of Mind: The Theory of Multiple Intelligences*. New York: Basic Books.

Gardner, Howard. 1999. *Intelligence Reframed: Multiple Intelligences For the 21st Century*. New York: Basic Books, p. 109.

Ponge, Francis. 1974. *The Voice of Things*. Translated by B. Archer. New York: McGraw Hill.

Thoreau, Henry David. 1950. *Walden: And Other Writings*. Edited by Brooks Atkinson. New York: The Modern Library, Random House, p. 125.

The Other Side of Knowing

Basho M, 1966. *The Narrow Road to the Deep North and Other Travel Sketches*. London: Penguin, p. 33.

Bringhurst, R. 1995. *Poetry and Knowing*. Edited by Tim Lilburn. Kingston, Ontario: Quarry Press, p. 52.

Dillard, A. 1998. *Pilgrim at Tinker Creek*. New York: Harper Perennial Modern Classics, p. 83.

Lewis, R. 1968. *Out of the Earth I Sing*. New York: Grosset and Dunlap, p. 21.

Lewis, R. 1969. *Journeys: Prose by Children of the English-Speaking World*. New York: Simon & Schuster, p. 170.

Thoreau, H. D. 1960. Journal entry, August 5, 1851. Quoted in *H.D. Thoreau: A writer's journal*, edited by Lawrence Stapleton. New York: Dover, p. 55.

Dreaming Into Waters

The children's poems in this essay are quoted from *I Can See the Air: Writings by Children, 1st/2nd Grade, East Village Community School*, Roberta Valentine, Classroom Teacher, Spring, 2005, published by The Touchstone Center as part of its arts and education project Air, Water, Light.

Bachelard, Gaston, 1988. *The Right to Dream*. Translated by J. A. Underwood. Dallas, TX: The Dallas Institute, p. 28.

Lewis, Richard, 1979. *Air Sings, Earth Dances: A Celebration of the Elements*. New York: Touchstone Center. Adaptation of a myth found in *Seven Arrows* by H. Storm, 1985. New York: Ballantine.

Shepard, Paul, 1999. *Encounter with nature: Essays by Paul Shepard*. Edited by F. Shepard. Washington, D.C.: Island Press, p. 13.

Watts, Alan, 1975. *Tao: The Watercourse Way*. New York: Pantheon, p. 90.

What Trees Know

Lewis, Richard, 2005. *A Tree Lives*. New York: Touchstone Center Publications.

Basho. 1966. *The Narrow Road to the Deep North and Other Travel Sketches*. Translated by Nobuyuki Yuasa, Baltimore: Penguin, p. 79.

Bachelard, Gaston, 1969. *The Poetics of Reverie: Childhood, Language and the Cosmos*. Translated by Daniel Russell. Boston: Beacon Press, p. 116.

INDEX